Animals as Friends

Sally Morgan

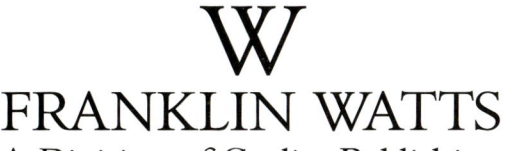

FRANKLIN WATTS
A Division of Grolier Publishing
NEW YORK • LONDON • HONG KONG • SYDNEY
DANBURY, CONNECTICUT

Picture Credits:

Cover: Rex Features

Interior Pictures: Ardea pp. 4 (Ian Beames), 11b (John Daniels), 12 (John Daniels), 13b (John Daniels), 25b (John Daniels); Bubbles pp. 5b (Denise Hager), 9t (David Robinson), 9b (Michelle Garret), 16t (David Robinson), 24t (David Robinson), 29t (Ian West); Camera Press p. 27b (Kathy Amerman); James Davis Travel Photography p. 17b; Ecoscene p. 8 (Stephen Coyne); Bruce Coleman pp. 17t (Julie Fryer), 18t (Jane Burton), 19t (Jane Burton); Robert Harding p. 22 (G. Roberts/Shout); Image Bank p. 27t; Impact Photos p. 25t (Steve Shipman); Tracy Morgan Animal Photography pp. 19b, 23t, 29b; Natural History Photographic Agency pp. 5t (Daniel Heuclin), 15b (Trevor McDonald), 21t (Suzanne Danegger); Only Horses p. 13t; Oxford Scientific Films pp. 6 (John McCammon), 15t (Martyn Chillmaid); Rex Features pp. 7b (Peter Brooker), 11t (Chat), 16b, 21b, 23b (Nils Jorgensen); RSPCA pp. 7t (Angela Hampton), 14t (Angela Hampton), 18b (Angela Hampton), 24b (Ken McKay), 26 (Ken McKay); The Stock Market pp. 10 (Rob Lewine), 14b, 20 (Don Mason), 28.

Series editor: Helen Lanz
Series designer: Louise Snowdon
Picture research: Sue Mennell

First published in 1999 by Franklin Watts

First American edition © 1999 by Franklin Watts
A Division of Grolier Publishing
90 Sherman Turnpike
Danbury, CT 06816

Visit Franklin Watts on the Internet at:
http://publishing.grolier.com

A catalog record for this title is available from the Library of Congress.

ISBN: 0-531-14563-8 (lib. bdg.)   0-531-15403-3 (pbk.)

Copyright © Franklin Watts 1999

Printed in Malaysia

Contents

Animals as Friends...................................4

Good Company....................................6

Planning Ahead..................................8

Training Your Pet...............................10

A Healthy Life....................................12

Learning to Relax..............................14

Feeling Proud...................................16

A Sixth Sense?.................................18

Pets for Protection............................20

Saving Lives....................................22

The Way Home................................24

Saying Goodbye..............................26

Old Friends.....................................28

Glossary..30

Useful Addresses............................31

Index...32

Animals as Friends

Millions of people around the world keep pets. Cats and dogs are great favorites. Other popular pets include hamsters, goldfish, budgerigars, guinea pigs, and rabbits. Do you have a pet?

Wild dogs were the first animals that lived with people. They would hang around campfires at night and wait for scraps of food.

Gradually these animals got used to living with people. They became domesticated, or tame.

The dogs we keep as pets today are related to the wolf family.

Now there are lots of different kinds of pets. Some people keep unusual animals, such as potbellied pigs, stick insects, or snakes.

People like to own animals because they keep them company and become friends.

Unusual pets need special care.

Keeping a pet can teach us about life, too. Looking after an animal helps us to become more confident and encourages us to take responsibility.

Taking care of our pets keeps us fit and healthy. Our pets can also help to protect us.

It's exciting to have a pet of your own.

Good Company

Having a pet helps people to feel wanted — and not so alone. It can be comforting to see a dog with a wagging tail, hear a cat purring in front of the fire, or listen to the sound of a bird chirping from its cage. People who live alone find it reassuring to know that there is someone else in the house to keep them company.

Having a pet gives people somebody else to talk to — and it's usually someone who will always listen.

Many small pets, such as hamsters and gerbils, only live for a few years. A cat can live for as long as 20 years. Some animals, such as tortoises and snakes, have very long lives — they can live to be 40 years old or more.

Whether pets are with us for a short time or for many years, they are usually an important part of the family.

If you own a tortoise, it might even be older than your mom or dad!

Animal Anecdote

Wil Cwac Cwac is one of the oldest ducks on record.

When he reached his 25th birthday, his owners celebrated by making a special birthday cake with 25 candles on it. It was one of his favorites — sponge cake filled with cream.

Planning Ahead

Choosing a pet and taking it home is very exciting. It is the beginning of a new friendship. But looking after a pet is also a big responsibility.

Pets that are picked up and played with a lot soon become friendly.

Once a pet has been taken home, it needs to be looked after for the rest of its life.

It's important not to lose interest and forget about a new pet. Animals depend on their owners to bring them their food and water.

Many small pets, such as hamsters and guinea pigs, live in cages. Their bedding has to be changed and their food and water containers washed every day. Large pets need a lot of looking after, too.

Caring for a pet teaches us to take responsibility for others. It also helps us to practice organizing and planning our time so we can fit in *all* the things we want to do.

Ponies have to be fed, watered, groomed, and exercised. That's a lot to fit into one day.

Training Your Pet

One of the responsibilities of owning a pet is making sure that it is well trained. A well-behaved pet is much nicer to live with.

Training an animal can teach you a lot about yourself. You learn to be patient — it can take a long time for an animal to learn new things.

It's important to be consistent, always behaving in the same way. For example, you should always use the same word when you give a command, rather than similar words that could confuse your pet.

Training your pet can be good fun.

Animal Anecdote

Sparkie the budgerigar was taught to say 531 words, 383 sentences, and 8 nursery rhymes.

Because Sparkie was such a talkative bird, he became quite famous. He was asked to appear on many television shows.

Sometimes you might feel like giving up, but you have to be firm and make sure your pet does everything properly. Most importantly, you have to find time each day for your training sessions. How well your pet behaves will show how well you have done your job.

Housebreaking a pet is very important. The number of "accidents" it has is one way to find out how well your training has worked!

A Healthy Life

Some pets need a lot of exercise if they are to stay fit and healthy. Dogs must be allowed to run around outside to use up all their energy. They love to fetch sticks, run after balls, and go for walks.

Taking the dog for a walk every day not only keeps the dog fit, but can help to make the whole family fit and healthy too!

Going for a walk every day is good for you as well as your dog.

Horses and ponies need plenty of exercise. They should be let out into a field every day or taken for a ride.

Riding also helps keep people fit. The rider has to work hard — riding uses muscles in the arms, legs, and back.

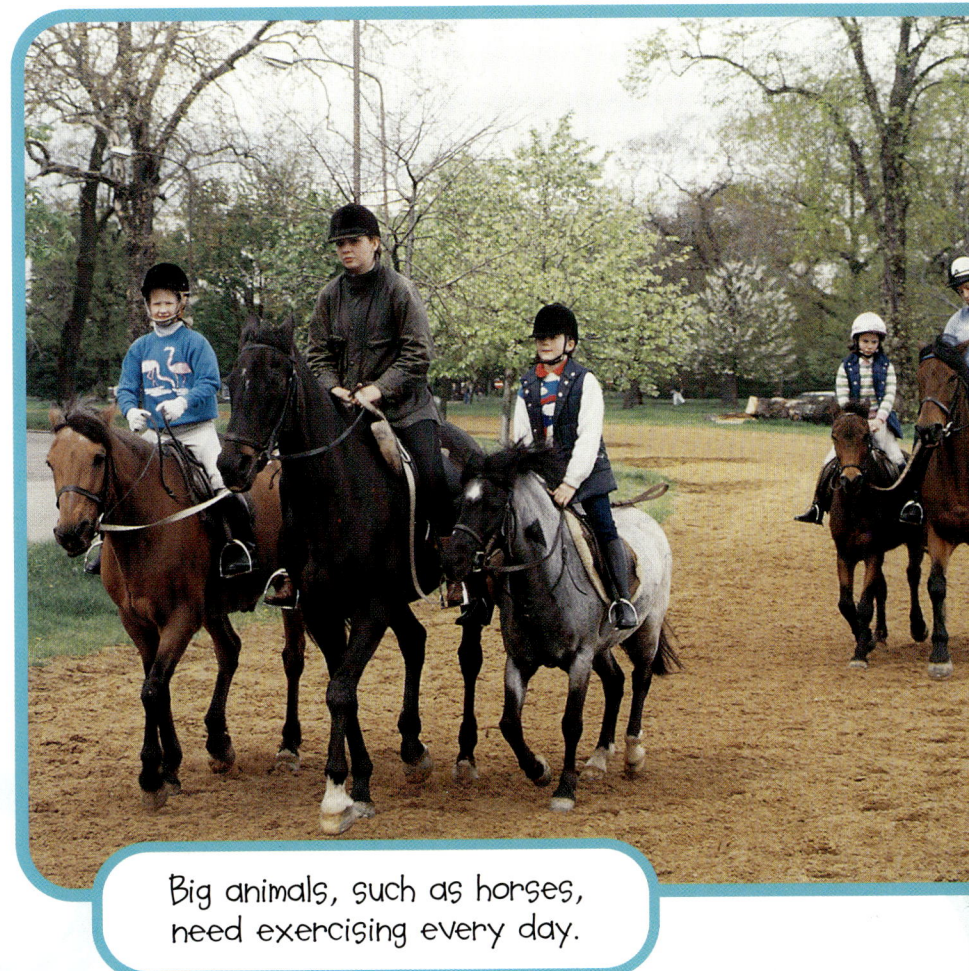

Big animals, such as horses, need exercising every day.

Give your pet plenty of toys, and also play with it yourself. The more time you spend with your pet, the better you get to know it. People find that playing with an animal is very relaxing, as well as fun.

Toys help make your pets' lives more interesting.

Learning to Relax

There are many things that can make people worry. Sometimes it's because we don't feel well, or because we have to take an exam, or start at a new school or job. Owning and caring for a pet can help us relax and keep calm.

When people stroke or talk to their pets, they become much more relaxed. While they are thinking about their pet's needs, they forget their own worries.

It feels good to cuddle a purring cat.

Scientific tests show that looking after and stroking pets can improve people's health.

Often, elderly people in hospitals or nursing homes cannot keep pets. Some pet owners take their animals to visit so the patients still get the benefit of being able to stroke and talk to animals.

Taking care of a pet gives people something to think about.

The calming effect of animals helps people in other ways too.

Some people get nervous when they visit the doctor or dentist. Scientists found that putting an aquarium (fish tank) in waiting rooms helped patients relax. They watched the fish swimming around and forgot about worrying.

Feeling Proud

Most pets need to be groomed regularly. Grooming helps keep your pet healthy, and it makes it look good, too.

Grooming your pet is fun. You soon become an expert hairdresser!

Many people like to enter their pets in pet shows. There are often prizes for the best groomed pet, the strangest pet, or the dog with the "waggiest" tail.

There are many proud owners hoping to win a prize at this cat show.

Winning a prize at a pet show is very exciting. It is a reward for all the hard work you have done to keep your pet healthy and well. Winning a prize can also make you feel proud.

Animal Anecdote

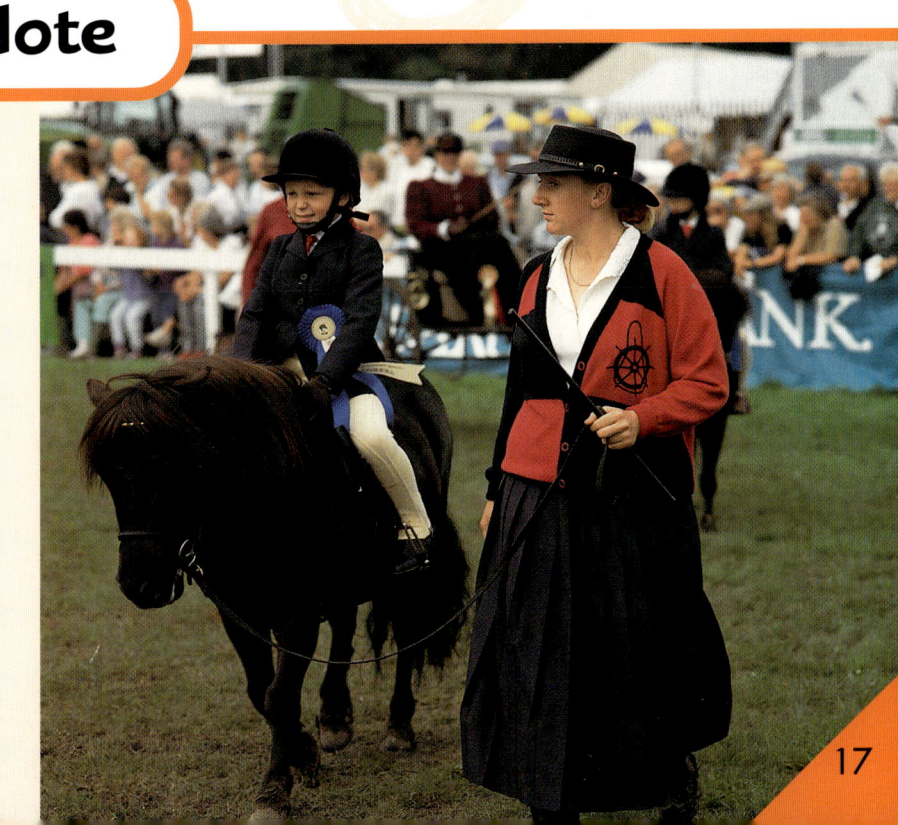

"On the day of my first pony show I spent all morning brushing my pony so he was all shiny. When we got to the show I was really nervous — I started to shake. I couldn't believe it when we won a prize. I was really happy — but I was still shaking!"

Anna, aged 8.

A Sixth Sense?

We have five senses — sight, smell, hearing, taste, and touch. But many animals sense things that we cannot. Mice and cats feel the tiniest vibrations in the ground and hear sounds too high for us to hear. Some animals are very good at seeing in the dark, when we can see very little, or can smell things that we don't notice.

Cats can see well in the dark.

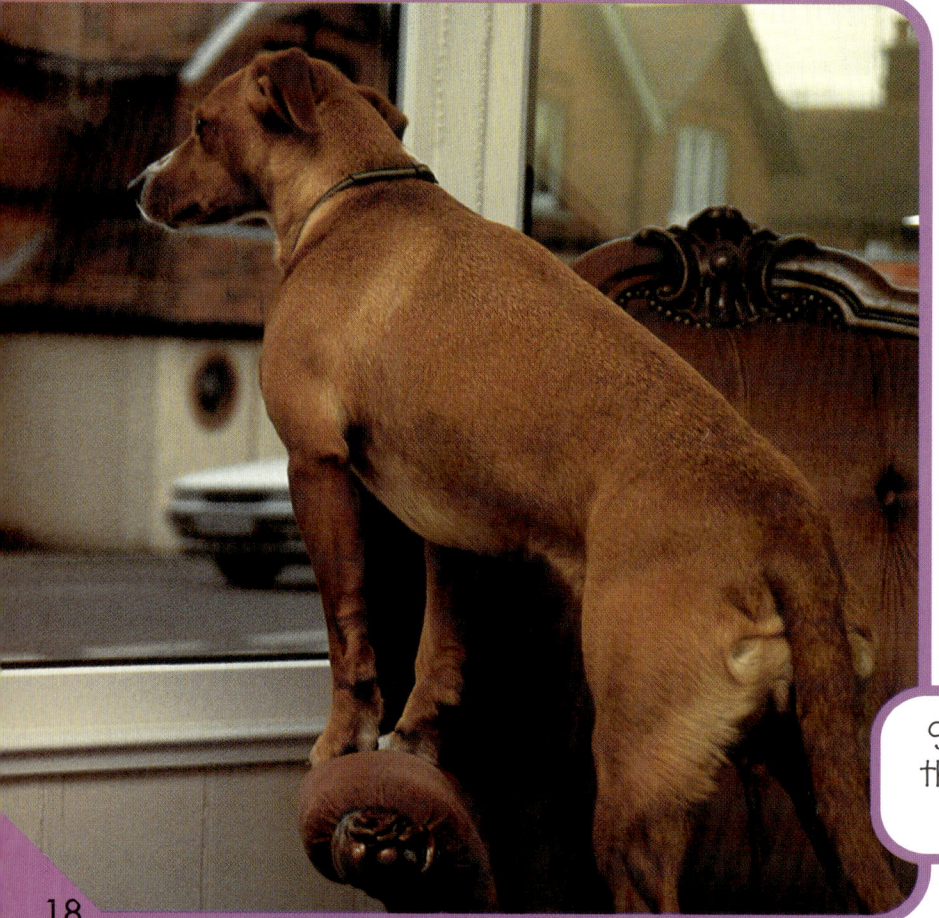

Some pets seem to know when their owners are coming home. They wait by the door or look out of the window. Scientists don't know how animals can sense their owners' return. Perhaps they have an extra sixth sense?

Some pets are able to tell when their owners are going to return home from vacation!

Sometimes the way animals can sense things we don't notice can protect people. Some animals can feel changes that mean danger. By watching their pets, people living in an earthquake zone may get an early warning before danger strikes. Many animals start running to and fro, calling out and trying to get out of buildings.

If a pet behaves in an odd way, it may be trying to warn us of danger.

Animal Anecdote

Thomas the cat lives with his owner, May, in Florida. One day Thomas was restless and wouldn't eat. Early the next morning, he woke May by scratching her face. May decided that Thomas was trying to warn her about something, and together they left the house.

Just one hour later there was an earthquake and the house was destroyed.

Pets for Protection

Animals are often used to protect us. Large dogs can be frightening. This is why certain breeds, such as German Shepherds, Dobermans, and Rottweilers, are used as guard dogs. They patrol buildings and industrial estates.

The family dog can help protect us and our homes. A barking dog will help scare off unwanted visitors.

A fierce-looking dog will stop even the bravest person in their tracks.

Some guard animals are more unusual. Geese can be quite fierce. Male geese, or ganders, can be very frightening when they run toward you with their heads down and wings out. This makes them good at guarding a house or farm. Their honking and hissing can be heard for some distance.

Geese hiss and even spit! They can look very frightening.

Animal Anecdote

Pigs have a very strong sense of smell. When pet pig Snort smelled gas leaking from a gas tap, she alerted her owners by oinking and running around. Her owners called the fire department, which traced the leak. Snort was given an award for helping to stop an explosion and saving her owners' lives.

Saving Lives

Pets and their owners can become very close. Sometimes the friendship between a pet and its owner is so strong that if something happens to the owner, the animal will try to help.

Dogs may go for help when their owners have had an accident. They bark at people to attract attention. Rescuers then follow the dogs to where their owners are lying hurt.

A barking dog can attract attention when there is a problem so help can be called.

There are stories, too, of horses who have gone for help when their riders have fallen off. The horses have returned to the stable yard and raised the alarm.

Horses sometimes help their injured riders.

Animal Anecdote

Fen, a border collie, was a friendly and lovable dog. His owner, Matt, enjoyed sailing. He often took Fen out on the boat with him. One day, Matt slipped and fell into the water. Fen was quick to leap into the water after him to pull Matt to safety.

The Way Home

The friendship between owner and pet can be very special. There are many stories of animals that have become separated from their owners and yet have managed to track their owners down.

People and pets can be such good friends that they don't like to be apart.

Sometimes when people go on vacation, they leave their pets to be cared for, in a kennel or cattery for example. Some animals manage to escape and find their way back home, even when it means traveling a very long way.

Pets may go into special homes while their owners are on vacation.

Homing pigeons are amazing birds. They become very attached to their homes and owners.

When they are freed, they do not fly off into the wild. Instead, they return to the loft, where they live and are cared for.

Homing pigeons can be released hundreds of miles from their home and still manage to find their way back.

Animal Anecdote

Sugar the cat was born in California. When she was two years old, her owner had to move 1,500 miles to Oklahoma. Sugar was left with a friend. Very soon Sugar was missing — it was thought she had died. Then, 14 months later, she turned up in the garden of her old owner's new house. Somehow she had followed her owner across the United States to a place she had never even visited.

Saying Goodbye

There are times when people have to say goodbye to their pets: People may move from one country to another and may not be able to take their animals with them; children who have their own ponies will have to sell them when they grow too big to ride them.

Sometimes pets become ill and die. It is very sad when a pet dies, especially if it has been part of the family for many years.

Saying goodbye to a pet can be one of the hardest things a person has to do, but it is part of the responsibilities of being a pet owner.

Many older people worry about what will happen to their pet if they die. They may ask a friend to look after it.

The strong feelings that some people have for their pets is shown when they leave money in their will to make sure that their pets will always be cared for.

Animal Anecdote

One of the richest dogs in the world is named Gunther. He was left £40 million by his owner.

Gunther lives in Italy where he is very well looked after. He has a car and chauffeur to drive him around the countryside and take him for walks. He also owns a local football team!

Old Friends

Many pets, whether they are large or small, become an important part of the family. The family grows up with its pets, getting older together.

The animals take on a very important role — always being there for comfort and company, seeing their owners through happy and sad times.

If you own a pet, you are the most important person in that pet's life and probably its best friend. In return for being well looked after, pets give their owners endless love and affection. And sometimes, people may even owe them their lives.

Animal Anecdote

Philip has had Toby since he was a puppy — they have grown old together. One day, as Philip and Toby were on their daily walk, Philip stumbled and fell — and he didn't get up. Toby nuzzled Philip to wake him up. When Philip didn't move, Toby barked and barked. He attracted the attention of other people, who came to the rescue.

Philip is proud of his dog. "Toby and I have been friends for a long time. He saved my life."

Glossary

affection — a feeling of liking or love.

comforting — when something makes us feel relaxed and happy.

companion — a friend.

confident — when you feel certain about what you are doing and believe in yourself.

consistent — not changing; doing the same thing.

dependence — looking to someone else to do something for you.

domesticated — when something has become used to living with people; when it has been tamed.

grooming — the action of looking after something; making it look neat.

loft — the space under a roof in a building.

patrol — to walk around an area and keep guard.

proud — when you feel pleased with yourself or someone.

responsibility — when you have to take care of something or carry out certain duties.

Index

affection 29

birds 6
budgerigars 4

cats 4, 6, 7, 14, 18, 19, 24, 25
chauffeur 27
companion 28

dogs 4, 6, 12, 20, 22, 23
  being domesticated 4
  on patrol 20
ducks 7

earthquake 19
exercise 12, 13

fish 15

geese 21
gerbils 7
grooming 9, 16, 17
guinea pigs 4, 9

hamsters 4, 7, 9
horses 13, 23

pets
  as friends 5, 22, 24, 28
  calming effect of 14, 15
  care of 8, 9, 16
  giving comfort 6, 28
  giving confidence 5
  responsibility for 5, 8, 9, 10, 26
pet shows 16, 17
pigeons 25
  pigeon loft 25
pigs 5, 21
ponies 9, 13

rabbits 4
rescue 22

sixth sense 18, 19
snakes 5, 7
stick insects 5

tortoises 7
training 10, 11

vibration 18

Useful Addresses

American Humane Association
63 Inverness Drive East
Englewood
CO 80112-5117

http://www.americanhumane.org/

ASPCA
The American Society for the Prevention of Cruelty to Animals
424 East 92nd. Street
New York
NY 10128

http://www.aspca.org/

American Veterinary Medical Association
1931 North Meacham Road
Suite 100
Schaumberg
IL 60173

http://www.avma.org/

PETA
People for the Ethical Treatment of Animals
501 Front Street
Norfolk
VA 23510

http://www.peta—online.org/

The largest animal rights organization in the world.